Funneling Your Way Through Composition

Lynn M. Patarini

Cover design by Grateful Publishing.

GRATEFUL
PUBLISHING

"We are what we repeatedly do. Excellence therefor, is not an act, but a habit."

Aristotle

Preface

This book is a guide to produce college-level writing. Based on my ten-plus years' experience, most freshman writers start college underprepared for expectations, especially in the area of writing.

Yes, most can develop a standard 5-paragraph essay, which is perfect for standardized testing. Yet when asked to think beyond question to develop ideas based on previous research, along with their own experiences, writers become stuck. Add expansion of those ideas through connection, explanation, and analysis, significant challenges develop.

Nevertheless, challenges are useful because challenges make writers think differently than in the past and maybe even push them out of their comfort zone.

Over the past five years, I have tested the various chapters in this book within classrooms at community colleges and four-year universities. The results have been more developed, thought-out papers that pushed my writers to grow both their writing voices and ideas.

Along the way, I have received valuable feedback from both students and colleagues. My attention to their input has assisted in the shape of this publication.

Here are some features that student writers have found helpful:

- **User-Friendly**. The book formatted linear yet can be used in any order. In most of my classrooms, we skipped around quite a bit. I take advantage of the idea to repeat chapters, such as the one on Revising, to further emphasize the idea that writers revisit their work more than once.

- **Overview of concepts**. Each chapter contains an overview of the idea and writer-friendly exercises to reinforce each part of the process.

- There is a separate **Multimodal section** to assist with understanding how multimodal communications impact our interpretation and decisions when composing. Also, alternative methods to brainstorm, outline, and compose to support organizing one's prose.

- Throughout the book, writers are prompted to **take advantage of on-campus resources** such as; writing and tutoring centers, research librarians, and professor's office hours.

- **There is an emphasis on writing as a process**. The book stresses the importance of revising and updating a thesis statement as a paper makes progress. The difference between editing and revising. Along with research first and throughout.

- The **Real-Life Applications** chapter applies the organizational and analytical skills of *The Funnel* to careers and everyday life.

These are just a few of the features that my writers have appreciated. I hope that future writers will have the same open-mindedness to employ these techniques beyond their first-year writing class to other coursework and, of course, life.

Let's analyze, organize, and, ultimately, communicate.

"Every part of the journey is of importance to the whole."

Teresa of Avila

Welcome to
Funneling Your Way Through Composition
This text will provide a guide to dive into a subject
and to write academically. How does academic
writing differ from everyday writing?
The central purpose of academic writing is to add
to an overall academic conversation instead of
repeating or reporting aspects of it.
Writers need to push beyond what others have
written to bring something new to an established
dialogue. To accomplish this task, we research
what others have written about a topic and then
looking at *what is missing?* This process involves
looking at another's theories from a different
perspective, building off already established ideas,
actually finding an entirely new solution to a
problem, and/or adding one's own experiences
and knowledge into the mix.
Whatever approach you as the writer decide, the
goal is always to bring something new to a
concept, issue, or idea to get beyond what research
is currently out there. This process is easier said
than done.

Here is a little bit about how this book functions:
Each chapter is a block building on the next, and
in the end, will help writers produce original
academic research. However, as writers will
discover, writing is not a linear process. Writers
may start at the first chapter yet jump around to
the chapters that provide the path to build a

persuasive paper. Suppose the urge to change topics happens mid-stream. In that case, writers will begin again to develop the research and analysis academic writing requires to complete the project.

Each step of *The Funnel* is explained in detail. The more familiar the writer becomes with each step, the higher the chance of this developing into a habit.

The Funnel Method can be applied to any college writing assignment and is adaptable for future employment needs. By mastering each part, writers have the skills to produce well-thought-out, provocative assignments.

Let us take a look at the general idea of each step:

Chapter One
Evaluating, Annotating & Interacting with Text

> "START BY DOING WHAT IS NECESSARY, THEN WHAT IS POSSIBLE, AND SUDDENLY YOU WILL BE DOING THE IMPOSSIBLE."
>
> ST. FRANCIS OF ASSISI

We start above *The Funnel*. As writers, we need to consider what our goal is for our paper and how we will accomplish it.
In other words, **let's plan.**
Take a look at the assignment. Here is the first place to start your evaluation.
Carefully read through the entire assignment. Before we begin, writers should understand what the professor is asking to be completed.

Look for keywords or phrases such as; evaluate, define, research, describe, explain, summarize, and or relate. Here are what areas the professor would like to concentrate on. In most cases, writers will be asked to formulate an argument of some sort.

When constructing this argument, keep in mind the basics of who, what, when, how, and why.
Who is your audience? (Think beyond just your professor – who could this research help in your community or field?).
What evidence is needed?
When is the assignment due?
How is your paper to be formatted? In the case of an English or Writing class, the answer is most likely M.L.A. Still, you may encounter other formatting in other classes, including A.P.A., A.P., and C.M.S.

Why did your professor give this assignment?
How is this assignment connected to the course objections?
Do not forget to consider the tone of your paper. Review your audience. Is this formal writing, or could the paper have a more casual voice?
At any point, if you are confused about the purpose of the task, ask your professor specific questions. (Never say, "I just don't get it." Try to develop explicit areas of confusion so your professor can clarify according to your needs).
Once the assignment's focus is determined, it is time to choose a topic and start reading. This process might be completed in a couple of different ways. First, depending on the assignment requirements, you may want to scan many different articles to get a sense of what is already researched. Once completed, look over the articles you found most interesting with a *mindful reading evaluation*.
What is a *mindful reading evaluation*?
You are currently reading this, yet your process may not be mindful. Let's consider a few questions:

- Starting with your environment - are you currently studying with friends or alone?
- Is the space quiet, or is there music playing or television blaring?
- Is your phone turned on?

- If you are reading this electronically, how many windows do you have open on your computer?
- Is your instant messenger turned on?

If you could answer "yes" to even one of the questions above, you are reading, yet there are distractions at the same time.

In other words, you are not reading mindfully. Mindful reading consists of micro-focusing, annotating, interacting with the text, and asking the content questions as you go.

Let us start with micro-focusing. Micro-focusing, by definition, is "capable of being focused on a minimal area.[1]" For our purposes, let us think of it this way, "focusing on a specific area of prose with a goal of a deeper understanding of the author's purpose or the content of the article."

How do we accomplish this?

We read actively. We concentrate on what we are reading by making notes as we go along. We start by highlighting the basics (thesis, main points, evidence). Besides, we look for words we do not understand to look up later.

The next step is to take a **believability evaluation** of the prose. Taking a piece of composition theorist Peter Elbow's Believability Game[2], we approach our next reading as if we believe every word written.

---

[1] https://en.oxforddictionaries.com/definition/microfocus

[2] https://scholarworks.umass.edu/cgi/viewcontent.cgi?article=1004&context=eng_faculty_pubs

- Go back to the thesis. Make margin notes stating why you believe this idea to be true.
- Now peek again at the evidence presented. Again, with margin notes, why are these sources perceived as experts?
- Lastly, let's examine the author's analysis. How is the author connecting the evidence and subtopic back to their thesis?

At this point, two phases of annotations should be complete. To oversimplify this process, note somewhere what you think is the core of the argument presented?

Also, note areas where questions arise within the writer's argument along with your statements. This should go beyond the areas you agree. Look at the parts that might be expanded.

Other areas to consider are what methods the author uses to get their point across. Aristotle came up with three rhetorical appeals: Pathos, Ethos, and Logos. **Ethos** refers to the credibility or acceptance of the author as an authority on the subject. **Pathos** is the emotional element within the argument. Lastly, **Logos** refers to the logical approaches the author employs. A good argument consists of a

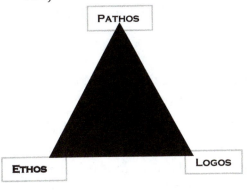

balance of all three of these elements. (See triangle example).

Annotating styles are personal since each of us organizes our thoughts differently. Some use multi-colored highlighters, while others might place post-it notes in the margins. (You may have noticed that the margins of this text are a bit wider to promote annotations).

So far, the reader has concentrated on what the writer is doing. There has not been any engagement or transactions within this essay. For our next step, let us try something new:

- Re-state the author's idea in your own words.
- Look back on your notes. Where does the author make their most persuasive argument? Explain why this is the most substantial element of the essay (in the margins).
- In your own words, why you think this way? Was this an experience? Prior knowledge?
- Lastly, note anywhere that could be clearer for interpretation.

Now let's consider contraries.

- Question what instinctually is not correct. This might be a direct statement that contradicts your experiences or a concept that challenges something else within the same argument. (Write questions out in the margins. Be specific). Make an additional note on any discrepancies based on your own experiences.

- Lastly, let us look into how the author presented his/her information. Are they using first-person? For what function? Are stories or examples presented in context to what you believe to be the overall goal of the essay?
- Where did he/she obtain their sources?
- What type of audience are they targeting? This task involves looking into where the essay first appeared. You might want to conduct a quick background check for the biases of the publication.

Keep in mind that a mindful reading evaluation is the equivalent of close reading.

Now get ready to annotate! See examples of each step.

Annotating – Thesis, Main Points, Source

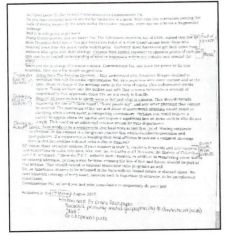

Next Step – Margin Notes, Believability

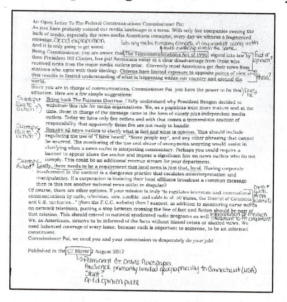

Phase 3 – Argument, Methods, Notes

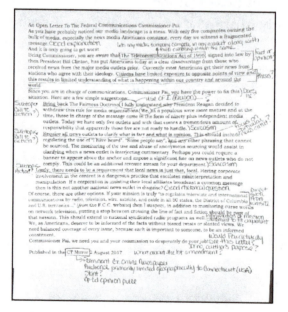

Applying these methods:

Read your chosen prose at least twice. Highlight what you consider essential. What is essential will vary somewhat for each writer because we all come from different places, cultures, and backgrounds. We bring our own conceived knowledge and head trash into how we interpret what we read, including our ethics, values, experiences, and prejudices.

Our next step is to question the author. What concepts have they presented that bother you? In your opinion, make the judgment of the validity of the overall argument? Where are the gaps? Make a note of any concerns. You may want to use an emoji to indicate where you agree. (I am partial to smiley faces, myself).

Checklist sample

- ✓ I read the essay at least twice.
- ✓ I made a note of the thesis and subtopics.
- ✓ I made notes of the sources used.
- ✓ I evaluated the essay based on what I know about the author's knowledge and background. (In this day and age, it is easy enough to look up an author to obtain additional background information. This step will assist in grasping the author's intent).
- ✓ I looked at where the original essay was published.
- ✓ I highlighted all the vocabulary I did not understand.

- ✓ I placed emojis next to the concepts I liked and those I did not.
- ✓ I placed question marks next to the concepts where I am confused.
- ✓ I made margin notes based on my knowledge to compare with the author.
- ✓ I have highlighted at least one quote that stands out to me to summarize the entire essay.

Each question mark poses an idea or two to write a paper. The author's thesis and notable claims may serve as evidence to tie back to another concept.

In a longer piece, take a look at each paragraph from this perspective. Decide the author's purpose in selecting this particular subtopic, evidence, and gauge how it fits with their thesis.

Once a complete, careful reading and annotation of an essay, academic article, or any other form of writing occurs, the analysis begins.

We start with standard rhetorical practices; author, publisher, audience, tone, topic, thesis, purpose, evidence, and finally, ask ourselves if the author met his or her goal for this piece of writing?

Just as we bring preconceived notions into our interpretations, the writer has also brought their views into their work.

Always take the time to look up information about the author's background. Are there any explicit biases towards the topic? Along with the same questioning, what biases did you bring while reading this editorial?

This exercise helps to discover why particular views of an author might cause discomfort for the reader.

It does not matter if you are trying to understand one piece of prose or many ideas from various authors. The approach should be the same.

Here we uncover the "gaps" in the author's theories, the questionable logic, or just an unfinished concept or theory. Every one of these areas is an opportunity for us, as writers, to expand upon, redirect, or question the conversation.

We look for ideas that interest us in assisting in engaging with our topic.

Side question: "What do we do if we are writing a paper for a class that is required, yet we have zero interest in the topic?"

The expected answer is to suck it up, act like an adult (trust me, future bosses will give tasks you will hate), and write the paper. The second answer is to think about the assignment with your ultimate goal, possibly your major, career, or personal life. Is there a concept or idea here you may connect to and explore? Keep in mind that this is about your present class. (It is dishonest to use the same paper in two different classes without permission).

Take your idea and discuss it with the professor who gave the assignment. Be specific. For example, if your English class has Human Rights as a theme, use a current topic or issue, say a debate about who controls local media. A debate you may find annoying. Of course, the assignment goal is to pull a concept then add it to the conversation. The latter part is vital, adding to the conversation.

Look for themes that connect to your interests. For example, a Computer Science or an Art major might not be interested in who owns what television station, yet with a bit of creative thinking, both could find a connection to the assignment.

The art major may ask, "What different approach from the essay could one take to limit fake news?" Then explore the essay from a marketing/creative advertising angle, looking into how the author used a protest to promote their cause. A Computer Science major might take another angle. They might use analytics to look at the demographics of people who believe certain ideologies, then show a connection to compare how the essay author used similar methods within their paper.

Review

When annotating

- ✓ Start by looking up the author's background along with where and when the piece was initially published.
- ✓ Find and highlight what you believe to be the author's thesis and subtopics.
- ✓ Circle all unfamiliar words or phrases to look up later.
- ✓ Write questions in the margins on concepts, ideas, or just places of confusion.
- ✓ Look at the evidence provided. Is the author using pathos, ethos, logos, or a combination of the three?
- ✓ How would you tackle this subject? Did the author miss any connections? Did they "bail" out on getting to the real issue?
- ✓ Ask yourself; what would you change, add, or expand in this conversation?
- ✓ Use this question as a guide to explore something new.

Here is where your paper starts!

Your answer to the last question becomes the lens for further study. Think of this as a limited view to go back and re-evaluate the original text.

Concepts & Terminology

Pathos: Using emotion within an argument

Logos: Using logic (facts and statistics) within an argument.

Ethos: The acceptance of the author as an authority on the subject by examining how they construct credibility.

Kairos: Timing of the argument with other events.

Rhetoric: the Art of speaking or writing effectively: such as the study of principles and rules of composition formulated by critics of ancient times. The study of writing or speaking as a means of communication or persuasion (Merriam Webster)

Rhetorical Concepts:

Audience: who is the intended end reader? Where and when was the original piece published? What biases does the publication or audience possess?

Purpose: Why did the writer write the piece; to persuade, educate, to inform?

Tone: Is the piece happy? Sad? Sarcastic? Fearful? What word choices did the author use to provoke these feelings?

Clarity: How is this argument organized? Does each sentence serve to help explain the author's purpose?

Organization: How is the paper organized? What connections take place between the main topic and the author's subtopics?

Evidence: What type of evidence is employed? Is the writer's argument more emotional (pathos)

than logical (logos), or do they provide a balance
of sources?

Writing Exercises:

- ✎ Annotate every source you read.
- ✎ Make margin notes at the start about why
  you chose this source and how it pertains to
  your vision.
  The more work you put into this phase, the
  smoother your path will be further into
  your project.

🏛 **Look in Chapter 13 for a Multimodal
approach.**

Chapter Two
Developing
Ideas

"I DWELL IN POSSIBILITY."
EMILY DICKINSON

We are still working above *The Funnel* utilizing information-gathering exercises. Taking the time to accomplish this helps us writers see where we can bring an idea into a conversation. This next step is vital.

Here we bring in our own knowledge about what we are trying to discover.

Let's review what we learned in the last chapter; reading actively allows us to microfocus on the text, highlight and question concepts within, and evaluate what the author is trying to show.

Now we need to take this to the next level and bring in what we (think) we know about the subject of the text. Like the author, we bring in our knowledge when we read. Our prejudices and preconceived notions show up when we do this, and that is okay.

As readers, especially of concepts we may not agree with, we need to keep an open mind. We seek an understanding of what the author is trying to say and why they think this is important. In other words: it is not always about us.

Nevertheless, in this phase, it is about us. Here our objective is to show an idea by using the claims of the original author. We need to look at their concepts (thesis, subtopics, conclusions), evaluate their sources, and then bring our take into the issue. Here we attempt to start to add something to the conversation.

Let us try this exercise: In one column, list what concepts stood out from the reading. Here you may want to incorporate exact quotes along with paraphrasing parts of the question.

In a second column, list what you know about said topics.

Furthermore, finally, in a third column, list what you would like to know about the topic.

Your chart may look something like this:

From Reading	Current Knowledge	What do I want to know?
The F.C.C. controls media. People cannot tell the difference between news and opinion. Local news should be local.	I get news from my social media feed. I generally agree with what I read. My grandparents watch the news on tv.	Am I getting news or opinion? Could this problem be solved through social media? What is the job of the F.C.C.?

Now we have three columns of information. Where do you and the author agree or somewhat look at the topic the same way? How does the author show these ideas? What evidence is present? (You may want to start a new list of just these ideas)

Now let us look at where you and the author do not agree or skepticism about the presented information.

How are your ideas different?

Does any of this fall into the 'what you would like to know' column?

Most importantly, what questions remain?

The last question question's answer may have the potential to add to the conversation, which is the point of academic writing. We do not want just to accumulate the ideas of others within the same paper. We want to bring in our own thoughts and ideas.

This form might be a different twist on what is already there by taking another's idea in a different direction. It might be an explanation about why someone's conclusion is misdirected. It might be taking what another has written and literally adding on where they stopped.

The key here is to bring **you** into the conversation.

- ✓ Explain the author's knowledge through the lens of what your knowledge is on the subject.
- ✓ Consider the concept of "adding to the conversation."
- ✓ What questions remain?

The questions become our starting point. Here are curiosities come alive, yet we need to look at what we are questioning.

- Are any of our questions obvious? Today, for our purposes, let us think of the obvious, "the duh-factor," as boring. We are searching to expand a conversation by making our readers think about a topic differently.

- Now that we have eliminated the obvious, what remains? Evaluate based on your limitations. Ask yourself, how could I develop "something new" from this?
- The "something new," whether an observation, addition, re-evaluation, or something else, will become your new lens.
    - Word this in a question format, then go back and look at your evidence. What parts connect? How do the other parts relate? How does this help "answer" my question? (Remember obvious is boring!) Furthermore, here is the big one: What do I know about this topic? Your knowledge positioning is with what you have and what you want to show.

Confused?

Let's look at an example.

Based on the text from chapter one, I question why if someone is lying (fake news), there is no recourse or is lying a matter of opinion. Here is a reference back to the viewpoint that news organizations should be more regulated.

From the letter to the editor and my knowledge, I know:

The Telecommunications Act (1996) changed how the media business operated.

The author wants the Federal Communications Commission to somehow "police" the news.

The author thinks that as is, the news is limiting the information people receive by slating it.

The evidence provided in the letter would need more research to understand completely.

The author's purpose may be something other than policing the news industry for error.

Should the government monitor the opinions of the news media?

What about 1st Amendment rights?

Where do ethics play a part?

At this point, we are working our way into *The Funnel*.

Exercises:

If your professor assigned a broad topic:

- 🖎 Take a look at what you find intriguing and make a list.
- 🖎 Then make a second list of what you already know about the issue. This could be based on your experiences, classroom discussions, or other authors you have read.
- 🖎 Make a second list of what you would like to know.
- 🖎 Where do your two lists connect? By looking at what is already known, a baseline develops. By looking at new knowledge, a possible opportunity exists to contribute to something "new."
- 🖎 Here is where you develop a starting question for research.
- 🖎 Keep in mind that most topics have a plethora of research available, especially with our ability to search on the internet. There might be an advantage to looking into an idea with a smaller lens. It allows one to get specific, detailed, and go deep within their ideas.

If your professor has the assignment starting with an essay:

- 🖎 Look at the quotes from your annotations; how do they connect.

- Write down the connection, then add your knowledge on the topic. Remember, too obvious equates to boredom.
- Develop this into a question. Here is a new lens to re-evaluate the essay.
- Look at what the author has to say about your specific angle. Would they agree or disagree with your view? How do they show this?

In both instances, the areas missing, the gaps, questions, places to expand each offer an opportunity to add to a conversation. In the next chapter, we get specific about research.

Look in Chapter 13 for a Multimodal approach.

Chapter Three
The Research Process

Here is the challenge many writers have: **research comes before writing the paper**. Most of us have got in the habit of writing out a paper and then finding the appropriate research that "fits" into our argument.

This is backward. We need to discover what others have said about our topic first to figure out where our concepts may work into the conversation. Here is a crucial step because if we are just compiling information from others, why bother to read our paper?

Here we are also working our way into *The Funnel* towards formatting **a working thesis**. A **working thesis** is a focused sentence that gives direction to proceed with your essay, critical analysis, or research paper and has the option to be rethought and changed as we discover more information. An actual **thesis** will eventually define arguments and summarize opinions.

So, where do we start?

Always look for sources perceived as being trustworthy. The first query should come from your college library's databases. This starting point gives the advantage of looking at credible sources from the start.

Take a look at your question. How can you condense this down to a "sound bite" of what you want to discover?

Put those words or phrases into the search. Here is where a vital lesson begins:

- No search results?
  - Rethink your topic.
  - Try different wording. Consider the essential keywords you would like to focus on.
  - Perhaps expand the scope of your focus a bit?
  - Alternatively, try a different way of saying what you want to know. **A zero result isn't a bad outcome. A zero result is another opportunity. As the researcher, you need to take steps to find out where your search falls.**
- On the opposite end of the spectrum, you may have over 5,000 results or more! Oh my! You have much reading to do!

Here you want to narrow your topic. The first step is to get more specific in your search criteria.

  - Skim some of the articles that surfaced. What do they have in common with each other, and with what you would like to know?
  - Start here to further develop and narrow down your keywords and phrases.
  - Once you have this narrowed view, continue your search. The more commonalities you find while

narrowing your topic, the more potential you have to focus your working thesis.

Always remember that we look at research first to find out what others have said about our subject. We are attempting to look beyond those who agree with our theory and those who do not.

We want to see where and how we might position what we want to write.

Narrowing Your Research

Start out with general search terms. Think about your topic, paper goal, and what exactly you are trying to discover. Be specific or you will end up reading a lot of research that has nothing to do with your topic.

Searching: Academic Search Premier   Choose Databases

Memes

AND ▾

AND ▾

Basic Search   Advanced Search   Search History ▸

Search Results: 1 - 10 of 29,520

Searching: Academic Search Premier   Choose Databases

memes and social media

AND ▾

AND ▾

Basic Search   Advanced Search   Search History ▸

Search Results: 1 - 10 of 245

Please note that by narrowing the topic just slightly, results get more specific.

When you narrow if you type in 'topic' and the word 'and' a list will appear. Take advantage of looking at the results through your lens.

Narrow your topic until the amount of results becomes reasonable to read and annotate.

Searching: Academic Search Premier   Choose Databases

memes and social media

AND ▾   politics

AND ▾

Basic Search   Advanced Search   Search History ▸

Search Results: 1 - 10 of 35

Limit to Full Text
Limit to Peer Reviewed

2012   Publication   2019
Date

Show More

Limit by Source Type

All Results
Academic Journals (26)
Magazines (4)
Newspapers (4)
Trade Publications (1)

Show More

Limit by Subject:
Thesaurus Term

Limit by Subject

Limit by Publication

In addition, consider limiting your search to specific dates, publication types, general subject and other specifics in order to get to the center of your discovery goals faster.

The ones who disagree are important beyond just a counterview. These writers provide opportunities for you to expand, add on, look at the topic from a different perspective, fill in the information, and, most importantly, **potentially add to a conversation**.

Here is a suggestion: in the beginning stages, if the amount of matching responses is overwhelming, read a few (let's say ten) abstracts or condensed versions to get an idea of what information is out there. There may be an opportunity to narrow your topic based on something interesting someone else started, or there may be a pattern where the information does not completely address the topic.

The part about reading was not a joke. Here we become experts on a subject by obtaining knowledge.

Once we narrow our topic, it does not matter if we are looking at full articles or abstracts; all should be read and annotated.

Here is why:

- The process helps us, as authors and academics, gain knowledge on a subject.
- It also assists us in keeping all the research straight, who said what and in what context.
- Some of this information may be used in our final paper. This is another opportunity to organize our research.

One way of organizing is to develop an **annotated bibliography**. An annotated bibliography is derived from each source we touch. This simple technique helps with the organization along with developing a Works Cited for your final paper.

- Start with a running list of each source. This can be as simple as naming each publication[3] with a couple of bulleted synopses.
- You may want to develop this list in M.L.A. (or A.P.A., depending on what you are writing) format.
- For each source, write a few notes evaluating the content.
- For easy references, provide actual, possibly useful quotes and page numbers.
- To take this a step further, provide a sentence or two after the quoted text to "remind" yourself how this all relates back to your working thesis. See sample on the next page.

---

[3] If choosing to simplify with the article name only, make certain it may be searchable for future citations.

Sample of a simple Annotated Bibliography:

New York Times Editorial – (Name & Date)
- Summary: Waterfront Homes from owner's view
- Biased
- "May want to insert actual quotes"

Hartford Courant Editorial- (Name & Date)
- Summary: Oceans are free
- Biased
- "Relevant quote"

CCSU Journal- (Name & Date)
- Impact study of land use by public domain (high tide marker to water)
- Significance of private beach on areas
- Environmental impact
- Economy impact
- "Quotes"
- Author notes/credentials

In the **research first process,** it is vital to avoid searching for research that "fits." This approach often produces the ugly quote bomb.

A quote bomb is a quote that fits into an argument just a little too well, almost as if it was written for it initially. Quote bombs do the work of proving a thesis. Suppose others have already proven a thesis or a concept. In that case, **your paper misses the point of adding to an academic conversation.**

In addition, the paper will waste the reader's time because they could just read the original work to learn about the idea. Or worse yet, your paper will be boring.

If you research simply to prove your point, you are missing the opportunity to learn something new about the topic.

The research phase of any project should be the most productive and, if done correctly, this portion should take the most time. Please keep in mind that this part of the research phase is only part one. Once we have a focused working thesis, there is a return round of evaluation with our new, narrower scope.

Research Checklist:
- ✓ Start with a question and use keywords within your library's database to search.
- ✓ From your search results, expand or narrow your topic as needed.
- ✓ Keep track of all sources, either by making notes on the front page of your printout or by starting an annotated bibliography. (A correctly formatted list of citations with a few sentences after each one describing the contents and how it relates or does not relate to your thesis).

✓ Once preliminary research is complete, narrow the question to develop a declarative sentence, your working thesis.

Exercise:

- ❖ Consider a topic that intrigues you. This could be anything from how to be an influencer to a method to avoid further climate change. (You might even want to do this exercise with an actual assignment topic). Now make a list of everything you know, or think you know, about this subject. Do not worry if the information is accurate or not at this point. Think in terms of "filling in the gaps" later with factual information.
- ❖ Find one view on your topic. The process could be a simple look at an editorial from your local paper or as sophisticated as getting an article from a renowned expert. Read, annotate, highlight, and comment on what the other person is communicating.
- ❖ Develop a list of quotes from your source.
- ❖ Explain under each how the quote connects back to your concept.
- ❖ Now relate this idea back to the knowledge that you bring to the topic. How does this all connect to what you want to know?

- ❖ Re-evaluate your notes. What have you missed? Did you oversimplify your argument?
- ❖ Finally, list what you still want to know. Where is the opportunity for exploration?
In the next chapter, we will take this information and develop our working thesis.

The Lion & The Statue

A man and a lion were discussing the relative strength of men and lions. The man contended that he and his fellows were stronger than lions by reason of greater intelligence. "Come with me now," he cried, "and I will soon prove that I am right."
The man took the lion to a public garden and showed him a statue of Hercules overcoming the lion and tearing his mouth in two.
"That is all very well," said the lion, "but proves nothing, for it was man who made the statue."

Aesop

Chapter Four
Developing A
Working Thesis

> "WE DON'T PRACTICE UNTIL WE GET IT RIGHT. WE PRACTICE UNTIL WE CAN'T GET IT WRONG."
> GINO AURIEMMA

The Working Thesis

The concept of a working thesis is simple; your thesis statement is not final until you hand in your final paper. Up to that point, writers are encouraged to modify, tweak, review, and even rewrite their thesis statements.

Remember, as an academic writer, your goal is to bring something new to the conversation. If this idea is approached without flexibility, frustration levels will explode. (The author cannot guarantee that this eliminates frustration, only that taking this attitude may help.)

Where do we start?

Consider your original question with what others have said:

- ❖ Who already agrees with your concept?

  If your paper does nothing more than agree with previously written views, your paper will be boring, both to write and those who have to read it.

If this happens, there are still tactics to move forward:

Because one has to be aware of any "head trash" they have leftover from a personal experience. The trick here is to be open-minded. As a writer, it is essential to recognize when an opposing view might be valid.

Now we get to the good parts. You have already developed a question for your paper to answer as a base for researching the topic.
Now let's push our query further. Our question needs to be complex enough to be interesting.
For example, *how does advertising affect body image?* Might have potential yet to answer it with *Advertising harms body image,* would be the "duh factor," or in other words, far too obvious (and boring!).
Instead, you might ask, *how does one's body image affect their shopping habits?* Then turn it into *A person who has a negative body image is more influenced by temporal fashions to solve their issues than someone confident.*
Another way to approach this is once you have the question, turn it into a statement, then ask yourself:
What do I want my readers to know? This portion should be the statement in front of you.

Why is it important for my readers to know this? Here is where the potential to add and bring a new idea to simmer together.

There may be other considerations such as:

Who is my audience?

What do they know about this subject?

What is my purpose (or goal) for this essay to accomplish? (Attempt to think beyond getting a good grade for turning in a paper).

Use the above as a checklist to make sure your paper will go beyond the obvious, or to put it more direct, be intriguing instead of boring.

Exercises (Some are completed in the previous chapter for use here).

- ✓ Take a look at the research list you have started. What stands out? Where can you add, expand, re-evaluate, redirect, and develop some part that adds something new?
- ✓ Now ask yourself; what question(s) remain? Search based upon the remaining questions to see what "experts" are writing?
- ✓ Write this down and re-evaluate your research within this lens.
- ✓ Add in your own perspective/experience. How is this an opportunity to add to the conversation?
- ✓ Here is your new question. The answer to this question becomes your working thesis. In the next section, we get into building our argument with subtopics.

🏛 **Look in Chapter 13 for a Multimodal approach.**

Chapter Five
Making Subtopic & Evidence Choices

Congratulations! At this point, you have a working thesis, the start of your research, your knowledge, and the potential for a great argument.

The Working Thesis

Now is the time to develop a path for your reader to understand your thesis is a clear connected process.

This section introduces various ways of organizing your thoughts. Each writer reading this most likely has their method that, hopefully, has worked in the past. Let us not think about what follows as abandoning the tried and true. Instead, consider this an opportunity to expand our horizons.

First, back to our lists. Where does the present research stop? Make a note next to each source that shows its relationship to your thesis. Ask yourself, *is this helping or hurting my argument? How do the author's ideas relate to what I am attempting to show?* The answer might be as simple as *Joe Researcher looks at my issue like this. I am expanding on his work by stating that.* Keep in mind that your subtopics help the reader understand your argument and ultimately play a part in influencing your reader's interpretation of your writing.

Take each quote/thesis note section. What are you ultimately showing here? Write this down.

Here is the start of a subtopic. Keep going through all your research. After you have this mapped out, it might look like this:

- Topic Sentence – describes the subtopic.
- Your evidence. Use an exact quote or example.
- Analysis – How does this relate to your thesis. In multiple sentences, explain the importance of the above in the context of your thesis.

Now scrutinize each paragraph's purpose through the lens of appeals (pathos, ethos, logos). This exercise helps to produce a balanced argument. Depending on the author's relationship to their topic, the more passionate the relationship, the more pathos seeps into the evidence. Be aware of this since one of the goals of producing a persuasive argument is to appear credible to readers. Suppose an argument relies too much on emotional examples. In that case, it may be more easily dismissed by those who do not share your views.

As in past chapters, the more detailed your writing steps are early on, the smoother the transition to a completed paper.

Exercises

- ✓ At this point, there is a lot of information to take in.
- ✓ Group like themed information together. Bring in logos (quotes and statistics from experts), pathos (the emotional component of your topic), and ethos (your knowledge and credibility as the writer) under each group.
- ✓ From here, write out a single sentence that summarizes what each group of information does to help a reader understand your thesis.
  - o The summary statements may work as topic sentences for each subtopic.
- ✓ Along the way, continue to evaluate all your information in the scope of your thesis.

Chapter Six
Analyze
Don't
Summarize

"WHEN EVERYTHING SPINS TIGHTLY AROUND A THESIS, THE PAPER IS POWERFUL. THE LESS SPIN OF INFORMATION, THE WEAKER THE PAPER UNTIL IT GOES FROM A HURRICANE TO A TROPICAL DEPRESSION. THEN I GET DEPRESSED READING IT."
PROFESSOR KELLY JARVIS

The Working Thesis

According to Merriam Webster, the definition of analyzing is "to study or determine the nature and relationship of the parts of (something) by analysis, which is a detailed examination of anything complicated to understand its nature or to determine its essential features: a thorough study.[4]"

For our purposes, consider the "relationship of its parts" as our (working) thesis. A "detailed examination" is how each part relates to our thesis. When we focus on our explanation, the lens limits the temptation to stray beyond our subtopic or evidence. Furthermore, if you get caught up in the temptation to explore a deeper subtopic, consider it an opportunity to revise your (working) thesis into a more tightly focused direction for your project.

The number one question to ask during the analysis phase is, "How does this (piece of evidence, argument, fact) relate to my thesis?" Although some background summary may be warranted, depending on your audience, do not forget that the purpose of bringing in other sources and voices is to help your reader see where your ideas measure into the larger picture.

---

[4] https://www.merriam-webster.com/dictionary/analysis

Think about analyzing verses summarizing this way; when we summarize an idea, we take that concept and condense it down to a more concise version in our own words.

When we analyze, we relate the idea to other theories or information to extract meaning that might not be apparent in a first read. The main goal is to have our readers reach our conclusions rather than rely on the conclusions of others.

Here is where the detailed outline from the last chapter comes in handy. A detailed outline helps one see the "big picture" because the body paragraph components are all visible in one place.

Sample of a simple detailed outline:
If paper was started with a question, state the question here.
Working Thesis stated in a complete sentence.
For each subtopic:

- **State subtopic in a complete sentence**. A version of this will convert to your paragraph's topic sentence in your first draft.
- **State the evidence using exact quotes or summary statements**. You may expand on the evidence with a quote to assist with qualifying your source to your reader.
  ***For draft purposes, not the readers, the addition of type of evidence (pathos, ethos, logos) might be helpful when looking at "big picture" to present a balanced argument.
- **A third sentence that states how the evidences relationship to your thesis**. This portion will be expanded with detailed connections in your final.

Detailed outlines can easily be expanded into a draft essay while allowing the writer to see where subtopics appear in the organization of an essay. This part is essential because an organized essay leads up to a definite conclusion.

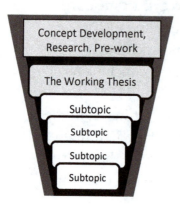

Again, consider the visual of The Funnel. Information gets more detailed and focused as information is presented. Worth noting is how the paragraphs are connected, with one leading into the next.

Your main objective is to show your thesis so readers comprehend the topic from your point of view and purpose. The reader should gain knowledge, perspective, and hopefully, appreciate your point of view.

Exercises

Here are some questions to ask when evaluating both subtopics and evidence:

- ✓ How does this relate to my thesis? (#1 question!)
- ✓ How am I using this evidence? Is it an emotional appeal or an example? Is it based on facts from a reliable source?
- ✓ How does this contribute to my argument?
- ✓ Is there any part up for elimination? (Think obvious!)
- ✓ What other methods can I use to get my point across?

After evaluating, this is an ideal time to start getting detailed in your analysis.

Chapter Seven
Re-Evaluating Your Thesis & Where to Start Your Paper

> "ONE CANNOT BE RIGHT UNTIL ONE REALIZES THEY ARE WRONG."
> DEREK BURTCH

By now, it should be evident to us writers that the analysis and evaluation of our paper's goals are ongoing processes.

Doing cognitive work in advance assists us with developing a bright, focused paper. No matter where someone is on their academic (or life's) journey, clear written communication is essential.

Let us take a look back at our working thesis and subtopics. We must ask, does the working thesis incorporate the entire argument of the paper?

If yes, how does each subtopic relate? This is part of the activity that connects each subtopic back to our thesis. Remember, here we are analyzing our materials through the scope of our thesis and making the connections for our readers.

What if we have concepts that do not directly connect to our argument?

Let's start with considering how do the missing idea relates somewhere in the paper? After all, at one point, we put this paragraph/quote/example in for a reason.

Here is where we put our writing egos aside and make a silent pledge to be honest about what we are attempting to accomplish. This is a difficult task to do, even for seasoned writers.

Why? We want to think that our ideas are right and our message is unmistakable.

Let's try an exercise:

Write one sentence that describes the crux of your argument. Try not just to rewrite your working thesis here.

Is your argument based on emotion, logic, or both?

How is this reflected in the paper? (Examples, credible sources, your own experiences, other methods).

Remember that part of our overall goal is to balance out our argument. A balanced argument assists with a reader who disagrees with your ideas based on a belief or an emotional connection. If your information is balanced, they still might not agree with you but may acknowledge your point of view as valid.

Here is a step in the right direction.

Now that we have made our evaluation, are there any parts that need adjustment?

Consider if the argument is too logical or abstract. Maybe start with why you are interested in this topic and consider where you might appeal to other people's emotions (pathos).

On the other side, how much emotion is present? Does the paper contain too many anecdotal examples and not enough factual information?

If this is the case, further research may be needed, specifically to look at what "experts" have written on your subject. The research conducted should start in your college databases and center on academic articles.

Academic articles often contain the most credible and least biased information instead of a segment on cable news or an advertisement. As a writer, you are looking at the facts, just the facts. Look for the most up-to-date information possible that may help your cause. Suppose you are using research that is more than five years old. In that case, you should justify the decision – where your question intersects with the research or how this author is the authority on the topic. Remember to read entire articles to understand the context and avoid the "quote bomb[5]"!

A quote bomb is defined as a quote that fits a little too well into your argument. The quote is doing the proving of the thesis, instead of the author connecting the evidence or example back to the thesis, through analysis, for the reader.

Quote bombs should always be avoided!

There are several techniques to avoid the quote bomb. One of the most utilized is to take advantage of the quote introduction.

Start with why are you using this person's particular words? The article author may be an authority in their field. Take advantage of his or her credibility by stating the author's name, the institution they are associated with, or where the quote was published, and then follow by the actual quote.

Suppose the expert is quoted in an article someone else wrote. In that case, the quote introduction might read, the author's name of the said institution was quoted in the media.

The point is to establish the credibility of the person being quoted upfront. On occasion, multiple quotes from the same author are necessary. There would not be a need to establish credibility with each quotation; however, each quotation must have some sort of introduction, even if it reads as simplistically as from (name of the article).

Remember to provide the analysis after each quote to explain to your readers how the quote correlates to your thesis. Never assume the reader knows why you are using a quote.

Now let us consider how this might be useful to look at other's techniques to emulate in your essay. At this point, we have read several pieces (essays, articles) by different authors. Let's look deeper into the approaches authors have used successfully.

What are the different devices used? Which techniques were incorporated? Let us make a list.

- One paper uses a famous quote that most people have read in another context.
  - How does this grab your attention?
  - What are the limits to using this device?

❖ Scrutinize where the agreements take place.
Is there really 100% harmony with everything written to date?

❖ Are there any areas of opportunity to expand, redirect, or re-evaluate any of the previously made claims?
Any of the above could be an opening to add something new to this conversation. It should be part of your assessment, particularly if there is a passion for the topic!

❖ What about adding a new twist? What claims made by others need further study?

With this idea, where does your experience fit into this?

❖ Let us think about the idea of personal experience. For example, let us say that you are writing a paper on social media harassment. During your middle school years, you experienced this first-hand, either as the harasser or harassed.
In either situation, your background adds a perspective that may, or may not, bring about a new way of seeing this problem.
First-hand knowledge is both an asset and a liability. As an asset, this helps as an evaluator of information. That same advantage is also a disadvantage.
Why?

- Another had related a personal story or anecdote.
  - How does this grab your attention?
  - What does the story do for the overall purpose of the paper?
  - What are the limits to using this?
- Another jumped right into their thesis.
  - Usefulness?
  - Limits?
- Yet another author started with a logical statement that relates to the thesis.
  - Usefulness?
  - Limits?

These are just a few of the many creative tactics one can use to get a reader interested in reading more. In your younger years, a hook into an introduction of subtopics leading into your thesis might have been the accepted pattern. Although the "bones" of this idea remain the same, introductions can get a little creative, depending on what you are writing.

No matter what choice you make to start, an introduction aims to provide a nibble for the readers of what they can expect in the rest of the prose. Based on the method used, this can be accomplished in one or multiple paragraphs. Your thesis should appear somewhere but does need not be the last sentence of your introduction – whoever is reading your work should know it when they see it.

In addition to your main argument, introduce some of the subtopics you will cover and how they relate.

You will dig into the details later as you break down each subtopic. Some of those details are already on your working outline; others may come to you as you are writing.

Just for fun, let us start writing an opening sentence for each of the previously listed introduction methods.

Let's go back to the annotated example we did in Chapter One.

I am writing a paper that extends my argument for government oversight for the use of fake news by major television networks. In addition, my argument extends to break up the big five, much like what was done in the telecommunications industry.

Here are several different approaches my first sentence could take:

- Use a famous quote.
  "It would be a gross understatement to say The Telecommunications Act of 1996 is not a model of clarity. It is in many important respects a model of ambiguity or indeed even self-contradiction." Supreme Court Justice Antonin Scalia

Example:

Your turn:

_____

_____

- A related story or anecdote.

Example:

Before the Telecommunications Act of 1996, newspapers funded investigative journalists. Reporters, like myself, took on the big stories. We worked with research teams to uncover corruption. My team was the first to be cut when my paper merged into one of the Big-5 media companies.

We knew that we uncovered one too many secrets.

Your turn:

_____

_____

_____

_____

- Jump right into the thesis. (This one would be considered "working.")

  Example:

  The Telecommunications Act of 1996 was just a corporate takeover of our federal government and should be repealed based on the illusion that the general public is getting factual information about world events instead of the biased views of said media corporation.

Your turn:

_____

_____

_____

_____

- Let us try a fact or logical statement that relates to the thesis.
  Example:

The mission of the Federal Communications Commission is "to regulates interstate and international communications by radio, television, wire, satellite, and cable in all 50 states, the District of Columbia and U.S. territories..." (*from* the F.C.C. website)

Your turn:

_____

_____

Although each sentence circles around one central theme, each sentence sets a different tone and a different set of expectations for the reader. Take a look at the various sentences you wrote. Which do you think your primary audience will most connect with? Explain the connection.

Ready, set, evaluate!

Look back at the Telecommunications Act examples. The first two might keep someone who already had an interest in this issue reading. Yet, they might irk another who made a lot of money off the mergers or no interest in the subject.
The latter two might be more universally appealing yet miss the mark in other areas.

- Think back to who is your audience?
- What type of language, word choice, and phrasing does your reader expect?
- Where do you make your best argument: with emotional appeal or logic?

Your answers to the above three questions will help direct your writing to the best place to start. From there, build your approach to the topic and incorporate your ultimate goal (a.k.a. thesis).

Remember, this is still only a draft – it is okay if your first idea does not work or if you still have unanswered questions. There will be plenty of time to appraise before finalizing.

Exercises

- ✓ Look back at your outline and add in a quote introduction for each piece of evidence.
  Remember to qualify the person you are quoting.
- ✓ Check over your "after analysis" to make certain you are connecting the materials in each subtopic back to your thesis.
- ✓ Ask yourself, does my thesis need revising?
- ✓ Review the techniques in this chapter for starting a paper. Choose the method that will assist the most with your paper's goal. You may want to draft a few sentences using the different approaches from this chapter.

Chapter Eight
The Revision Process
(most likely to be repeated more than once)

> "REVISION DOESN'T ALWAYS MEAN CONCISE. REVISION COULD MEAN A WHOLE NEW DIRECTION."
> JENIFER BAKER

The Revision Process (most likely to be repeated more than once)

Ah, the revision process.

If you are thinking, "but wait, my paper still lacks a conclusion and possibly some sort of counterview," you may be right, but if you think revision only happens at the end, think again. After each step, there lies an opportunity to re-evaluate our paper's goals.

There are many techniques to approach this section. It might be advantageous to use multiple tactics to craft this project into its best version. The challenge here is to be open-minded to edits along the way.

Let's start by reading through our papers. Ask yourself (and be honest, not lazy): Is my topic precise throughout? Could someone besides me follow my logic?

Most writers say yes to both questions in the last paragraph – but give it a hard look and find places where your reader might get lost. Where do you see the disconnect? Revise to connect or eliminate that area. Deleting is usually the most challenging task when you have a word count or page quota to hit, but better to cut the slack than fill your paper with filler. Taking out portions that fail to help connect your thesis will allow you to use your research and write a more focused paper.

This type of self-scrutiny is a valuable attribute when constructing reports for future employers or clients.

Revision includes rewriting. It is more than a grammar/sentence mechanic check, which technically is editing.

If you are having trouble with self-evaluating your paper, there are multiple options for assistance. The first would be to consult with your professor. Most have office hours and are happy to help students improve.

You also might try your campus writing center. Writing centers usually employ students, just like you, who have already mastered this Art. They will not fix your paper, yet they will provide suggestions to make it sounder. They will certainly empathize with the struggle of revisioning!

Another path might be to work with one of your peers. Peer reviewing is a crucial step when writing because it lets you see how someone else approached the same assignment and allows for advice from someone in a similar situation.

The key to peer review is not to have another "fix" your paper. Revising and fixing your paper is your job. Writers should make a list of their concerns. Your "reviewer" will consult this list when reading to concentrate on the areas you feel are soft.

The reviewer might also point out grammatical errors, yet this is not their function.

For errors in structure, try reading your paper aloud and make a note of any sentence that sounds awkward. One might also read backward. This approach makes your brain focus on every word, helping to catch synonyms, homonyms, and other word choice errors along the way.

Are you working alone?

Review the first chapter about how to read an essay. Why not take this approach with yours? The first suggestion for doing this is to clear your head. You are changing hats from writer to reader or audience. Do something else for an hour or two. Take a walk, get some food, anything to get your mind off this paper.

Upon return, sit in a quiet space. Take out a hard copy of your paper and make notes as you read—question your concepts. Underline areas that work. Make a note of ideas that others might challenge. (This comes in handy when evaluating for a counterview). Have you explained and connected those thoughts as clear as possible? Are you leaning more into emotion than logic?

After you complete this task, go back and revise for clarity.

Another option might be to do a reverse outline of your paper. Reverse outlining lets the author see where the paper has developed since the initial detailed outline, along with possible areas to elaborate further.

Are you a visual person?

A mind map might be the way to go. A mind map is just another way to look at your paper. To make one, start with your thesis or central idea in the center of a piece of paper, a whiteboard, or any surface you can draw. From here, use "branches" to show each subtopic. Then more branches to connect evidence, examples, and of course, your thoughts. Once completed, a massive spider-like drawing develops.

Here the paper's goal is in the center while all the proof appears around it. This visual works for some and is too much for others.

Always take the approach that works best for you!

Once the information is available to revise and make the paper more reliable, do it! Revision is a multiple-step process that may need to be completed more than once to get your paper to its most potent form.

Some of my most successful students end up rewriting their entire paper - multiple times!

Exercises

As writers, we are always experimenting to find what works best for us. Please try multiple revision tactics to see which ones work best for you.

- ✓ List your thesis revisions on the top of your essay. This allows you to see the progression of your paper.
- ✓ With your current working thesis, re-evaluate all materials. Ask yourself how each sentence helps the reader understand your paper.
- ✓ Take notes of vital areas.
- ✓ Also, take notes of areas where your reader might disagree or question your logic.
- ✓ Try to "think like a reader" during the revision process. Keep in mind you are going for a paper that makes sense to someone besides you.
- ✓ If stuck, try a reverse outline to compare to your original detailed outline.
  Where has your paper progressed?
- ✓ Revise, rewrite, reimagine along the way.
- ✓ Remember that revising takes place multiple times within the writing process. After all, revision puts the process in the writing process.

Chapter Nine
The Ethical Counterview

> "WHEN WE MAKE AN ARGUMENT, WE SUBJECT OURSELVES TO THE JUDGMENT OF OTHERS."
>
> JOHN DUFFY

Counterview

If we stick with tradition, then the **counterview of an argument** will be placed in the paragraph before the conclusion.

In the spirit of the same tradition, this counterview would explore the exact opposite of what your argument may be. It may start with "Although so and so writes this, we believe this," illustrating a very binary view of your issue.

As writers, we need to approach this portion more openly. The last chapter suggested reading one's paper as the audience versus the producer. After all, a significant part of critical thinking sees many points to the same argument. It is our critical thinking skills that allow us to analyze to understand. By using this skill set, we force ourselves to employ open-mindedness and, in the process, understand others.

One way to approach this is by asking, "what if I am wrong?" Alternatively, "what if my argument is not valid?"

Go back and inspect our paper like a reader—note areas where someone might disagree or question your theories. Alternatively, look at an area that could be revised (again) for clarity.

Once you have a set of both writer and reader notes, compare the two.

Ask yourself:

- How might you revise an idea to address and ease your reader's concerns?
- Decide if the concern is strong enough to address it here and now in this paragraph or if it should be brought up earlier or later in the paper?
- If the concern is strong enough, you may have to evaluate the entire approach the paper takes.
- If the concern arises in multiple areas, you may want to wait until the end. Traditionally, sandwich the counterargument between your strongest point and the concluding paragraph.

We want to unpack our assumptions and examine where our argument might gain or lose effectiveness by addressing these issues upfront. By listening to or reading another view, we are gaining further perspective on the problem.

Bear in mind that **bringing in another perspective adds to your credibility as a writer**. By doing so, we demonstrate a level of open-mindedness and an ability to acknowledge multiple views on a single issue. The balance of argument is significant when taking a stance on emotional topics that hit people's nerves.

The revision process only ends when you submit your final paper. Up until that point, every word is eligible to be changed.

Exercises
- ✓ Read through your paper (again) — this time, note areas where a reader might look at your statement from another angle.
- ✓ Note these areas.
- ✓ Write a sentence or two clarifying your perspective on each note.
- ✓ Now ask yourself-
  - o Should I explain this further here for clarity?
  - o Do I need to address this concern at all? By not acknowledging this concern, am I diluting my own argument?
  - o Finally, make a note for each issue, based on your opinion, of course, where this observation needs to be addressed.
  - o Do you acknowledge and move forward near the beginning?
  - o Do you bring up another viewpoint in the pertaining subtopic?
  - o Or do you just ignore the concern completely?

This all comes down to the choices we make to communicate our ideas.

Chapter Ten
Writing A
Kick Ass
Conclusion

"IF YOUR CONCLUSION ONLY RESTATES YOUR
MAIN POINTS AND YOUR THESIS, THEN YOUR
PAPER HASN'T MADE FORWARD PROGRESS."
DR. PAUL KARPUK

Conclusion

We are almost there! Not to add pressure on your project, but for writers, the conclusion to any paper is the most crucial paragraph, which is why waiting until the very end to compose it is essential.

The conclusion encompasses the entire paper and then pushes the reader further. This is one last attempt to get your readers to understand what you have written.

Traditionally the conclusion revisits the thesis, the main goal of the argument. Conclusions also highlight subtopics, and in the end, provide a statement to motivate the reader to further action.

All the good stuff!

At this point in any project, most students just want to finish. You probably are tempted to rush through the end like a fairy tale with, "and they lived happily ever after the end."

Cute yet not adequate.

Again, here we have one last chance to prove our thesis, reinforce our argument, and, hopefully, influence our readers to think a bit differently about our topic.

Whew! That is pressure.

Nevertheless, at this point in our process, most of the work is completed.

Remember way back when we reworded our thesis to a single idea? Take a look at how you went about doing this. Look at every reversion of your thesis from start to finish. Is your final sentence still appropriate to your argument? Or have you tweaked and revised your original so much that this is now unrelated to your paper's goal?

If still appropriate, let us start here. Re-statement of the thesis, check. Usually, this is not the situation.

If not appropriate, what is missing? Rewrite another sentence that expresses this to your reader.

Now we (again) assess our subtopics. In each paragraph, what is your strongest point? Consider each example, piece of evidence, or the connection of how it relates to the thesis. For each subtopic, state this information in your own words.

Nice job! In front of you sits yet another list, correct? There is one more step before actually doing the written work. Please re-read your introduction. How are you starting your paper? We discussed in an earlier chapter the various practices one may employ to start their essay. Touch on some part of this to tie your paper together.

For example, if one used the first-person narrative technique, continue the story here, or expound to connect it further with your thesis. We relate everything all together.

Now in your own words, connect the contents of your list, emphasizing the overall connection back to your thesis — the paper peaks at this point to influence your reader's view on your topic.

Other additions might be beneficial, such as offering a solution or posing the next step. It is a good idea not to bring in any new information at this time beyond a plan.

Your final challenge is to write an ending statement that will be remembered by your readers. The last sentence is what will resonate and most likely be what they remember. Take this opportunity to make one last attempt to draw attention to your perception.

Exercises

- ✓ Start with reviewing the progression of your thesis statement. If needed, revise.
- ✓ Evaluate the information in each subtopic. Choose the strongest element, whether this is your evidence, example, or analysis.
- ✓ Write this out in your own words.
- ✓ Since we want to strive for a balanced argument, you may look at your list and decide what sentences relate to pathos, ethos, or logos.
- ✓ Consider the order of your highlights. What are the most important, and which are just reminders?
- ✓ Compose a final version of your thesis. Please do not cut and paste from your introduction. Your thesis, like your paper, should make progress.
- ✓ Once your revised thesis and subtopic information is brought together, decide how you want to leave your readers. What final thoughts, calls to action, and last pleas do you want to make?
- ✓ Organize your information. Remember back in the Introduction section we read about multi-paragraph introductions? The same applies here. The goal is to end strong!

One other note – sometimes we compose a stunning conclusion. Yet, when read in relation to our entire paper, we realize that our current conclusion would make the perfect introduction.

When this happens, let out a deep sigh, and do what is best for your project. We have all been there.

Chapter Eleven
The Benefits of
Peer Reviewing

"CRITICISM, LIKE RAIN, SHOULD BE GENTLE ENOUGH TO NOURISH A MAN'S GROWTH, WITHOUT DESTROYING HIS ROOTS."
FRANK A. CLARK

The Benefits of Peer Reviewing

Our peers can provide us with a vast amount of knowledge, and knowledge sharing is a positive accomplishment.

Whether required by your professor or not, a peer review session can help with last-minute polishes to your argument (paper). Let us face it, after reading a paper over several times, one's mind has a more difficult time picking up sentence mechanic mistakes along with shifts in the point of one's argument. This is a common occurrence with both seasoned professionals and novice writers. Another set of eyes will pick up on nuances within a paper that the writer often misses.

However, there are other reasons to peer review:

- Peer review helps us writers see our work from a reader's perspective.
- Peer reviewing brings about a collaborative writing opportunity for multiple writers to work towards a single goal.
- Writers can see opportunities within their own papers by reading another's approach to the same assignment.
- Peer review assists in clarifying ideas within a paper.
- Moreover, finally, peer review minimizes last-minute questions by applying the recommendations of others.

Usually, at this juncture in our writing practice, there have been experiences regarding peer-reviewing, and not all of those experiences were good.

- Writers are uncomfortable assessing another's work or having a peer look at our draft.
- Writers believe the only feedback that matters will come from their professors.
- At other times, writers feel "cheated" when one provides detailed feedback while another receives only general comments. Suffice to say, not every student is capable of giving complete feedback to their peers. We have all felt ripped off by a colleague's halfhearted peer review or harsh comments.

Since every writing class is different, so is every professor's approach to peer-reviewing. Some will just have students exchange papers without clear goals in mind. In contrast, others ask reviewers to answer a series of specific questions. Whatever technique used in the past, keep an open mind when reading ahead. Not every approach will work for every writer.

Sometimes we need to combine two or three of the upcoming exercises to get the feedback we want. And know, that is okay.

The Basics

The simple way to peer review is to have another person read a paper and make notes in places where changes should occur. This method may provide acceptable feedback, yet both parties miss opportunities to improve their paper. To start, this limits the number of paper views. Even if this exercise extends to a third person, the latter tends to read the paper along with their predecessor's notes. This invites a simple view of one's work as it is easy to agree, be lazy, and not add another's opinion.

If the goal is feedback from multiple people, each participant should receive a clean copy of one's essay. Once the original author obtains all of their reviews, they can decide which advice to apply to their work.

The Basics Plus

As an add-on to basic peer-reviewing, we writers pre-evaluate our work using annotation to develop questions. These questions offer our peer reviewers a specific lens through which to evaluate the essay. The questions also provide parameters for the author to base their claim and offer the opportunity to create a tighter assertion.

Sample questions may include:

- Is my thesis incorporating what is in my paper?
- Do my subtopics connect back to my thesis, or do they drift off into their topics? Please show me the drift points.
- By reading my introduction, do you get a sense of what is to follow? What should be revised to accomplish this goal?
- The same could be asked about the conclusion along with the question, would my conclusion make a better introduction?

Students should note that none of the above questions ask the reviewer to line edit for mechanical mistakes. This task should fall primarily on the author. The occasional awkward sentence or misspelled word is reasonable, yet if a reviewer notes multiple errors in this draft stage, then the writer is not doing their part to produce the best work possible.

Beyond Basic

This approach is less comfortable for both parties. Here the reviewer looks at the paper as a product. They note areas of strength and explain in the margins why including;

- Dissecting word choices.
- Looking into source credibility.
- Considering how a source usage.
- And lastly, considering the overall goal of the paper.

Human nature tends to focus on the negative, so being positive may be a challenge for some.

Once an evaluation of all the good parts is complete, the reviewer should highlight and note in a way that will be clear for the author. Consider using emojis, a highlighter, or a method of your own choice, that will be different from the one used to point out improvement areas.

Now the reviewer needs to ask themselves why the other areas do not measure up. Here is where tact and word choices come in.

- Where is the disconnect from the paper's main topic?
- Why does the reader struggle to connect here?
- If appropriate, the review might make suggestions on how to clarify.

When one comments on something, anything, it is effortless to say it is terrible. The tricky part is to explain why something lacks.

From the author's perspective, criticism is hard to hear.

Some suggestions for an author during a peer-review process:

1. Check your ego. We all have one, and very few of us like when our weaknesses are exposed. Keep in mind that this process's goal is to make you a better writer.
2. Listen with intention. Take notes.
3. Do not justify your choices. Sentence mechanics need fixing. Difficulty understanding due to mechanics and misspellings are non-negotiable.
4. Know that all changes are in your power. If you do not agree with some of the suggestions made, do not do it. Keep in mind that when multiple reviewers suggested the same edits, the revisions should take place. If one person has a problem with a source or how the author worded a phrase, so be it, yet if two or more people point out the same challenge, strongly consider a change.

One last note- in peer-reviewing, as in life, sometimes one gives more than they receive. Always try to do your best, and if, in the end, the comments you receive are not useful, there is a choice.

- Ask your reviewer to re-read and look at specific areas. (This is where the questions come in handy).
- Ask your reviewer to explain their feedback further. Can you show me where you saw this (fill in the blank)?
- Have someone else read your paper and see if they come to the same conclusions.
- And finally, your professor should have a mechanism in place to provide reviews of your reviewers. If you are uncomfortable expressing yourself here, as many students are, have a conversation with your professor. Most likely, they know who the slackers are and will try to steer you into another situation for your next peer review.

Remember to be mindful that you are looking at someone else's hard work, and not everyone has the same capacity for criticism. Be honest, yet always combine honesty with kindness.

Student's goals by peer-reviewing are to help another peer write a better paper and possibly takeaway methods to help better their papers.

Exercises

Although the chapter gives multiple peer review
options, here are a few more to consider.

- ✓ The Gossip Session – One writer reads their
  work aloud to three or more reviewers. The
  reviewers listen and take notes.
  Once the writer is done reading, the
  reviewers compare their notes and read
  suggestions to the writer.
  Here is the difficult part, the writer cannot
  speak until the end and may only ask
  clarifying questions. The writer should note
  their reviewer's observations yet should not
  justify any of their decisions.
  This is more difficult than it sounds, yet the
  writer usually receives much usable
  feedback in the end.
- ✓ The Letter – Some folks are just not
  comfortable speaking their views or asking
  for help. The Letter Peer Review helps.
  The author writes a detailed letter to their
  reviewer(s) explaining where they need
  help.
  Reviewers read the letter and the provided
  draft and make notes pertaining to the
  author's concerns and any other
  observations they may make.
  The reviewer then writes a detailed reply
  back to the author.

Both the author and reviewer need to consider word choice and tone in their communications.

This method has helped many as rarely a reviewer will "write in" response because they put their thoughts on paper for anyone, including the professor, to see.

Chapter Twelve
Completing
The
Funnel

"LET'S TRY TO MASTER THE TASK INSTEAD OF CONCENTRATING ON THE SCORE."
ANONYMOUS

❖ Chapter Twelve – **Completing The Funnel**

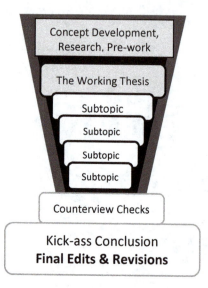

Here is the final step before handing in that essay, report, project, or any of the many other names both supervisors and professors give to assignments.

There are just a few more details to work out.

Now that your draft is complete, go back to the revision mindset for a final read-through. At this point in the process, do another pass-through to copy edit—concentration on spelling, sentence mechanics, paper format, and word choice.

Although a tedious task, there are times when the difference between an A paper and a C paper comes down to readability. Spelling and grammar errors are a lazy way to lose a reader's attention.

Remember to complete one final read-through. Check transitions to make sure your argument is connected. At this juncture, there is a possibility that you will not have significant changes as your paper ought to be reasonably polished.

Also, keep in mind that beyond the looming deadline, a project gets to a point wherein the writer's mind, you are done.

Think about it; you have developed, analyzed, organized, connected, revised, edited, and finally, finished your paper. After one last read-through, whatever you are writing is ready for submission.

Congratulations.

Take a deep breath, high five yourself, and hit that button, or do whatever you must to submit your work.

Chapter Thirteen
Multimodal
Approaches

"A PERSON WHO NEVER
MADE A MISTAKE, NEVER
TRIED ANYTHING NEW."
ALBERT EINSTEIN

We live in a world where the methods of communication change by the minute. The way we write progresses along with this intensity. We, as writers, must consider the best method of communication to achieve the goal of understanding your message.

Any book on writing must consider the multi-mediums and multi-methods used to communicate. The idea of multimodality simply means projects that have multiple modes of communicating a message. For example, traditional college research papers have one mode, text, to communicate ideas. In contrast, a poster would have the text and an image or graphic to deliver ideas to their audience. Of course, one might add in sound, video, and an array of other techniques to convey information, too.

How might this all work?

Let us consider a typical day. You wake up to an alarm on your phone, maybe to a favorite song or a direct connection to the day's news and weather (audio). The route to the college features temporary flashing signs with a text message, road signs with directional, maybe a billboard, or other forms of advertising.

There is a stop at a local restaurant for breakfast. Above the counter, a hanging television features the local news. Behind the anchor, photographs, charts, and graphs fill the space. They cut to a video of the event. All this time, a crawler across the bottom of the screen carries more information about the current, or maybe other, topics. Even a menu is a form of communication with food descriptions, allergy warnings, and maybe a family story.

There is background music that may be a calm instrumental or a current song that features social justice lyrics by Kendrick Lamar or a spoken word poem on a similar issue by Meta Sarmiento.

Once you arrive at the college, important correspondences are delivered through email, text, and let us not forget face-to-face communications.

The point is that at times a poster on a wall will effectively communicate a stronger message than a six-page essay, yet they both would contain similar information.

The composer must consider the mode of communication to best compose their message and, as discussed earlier, the potential audience. In 2019 one might not use a BLOG post to reach the highest number of senior citizens. Yet, an article in a local newspaper or a segment on the local news would be in many living rooms. Along with the same idea, choices still need to be made as far as type size, what information is essential to know, how you will explain why, and the shortfalls of your communication method.

This chapter will feature alternative methods to brainstorm ideas, organize thoughts, and produce precise, comprehensive results. We need to consider other ways to communicate because the world is more than 6-page papers.

Let us start with **Brainstorming.**
Brainstorming is a method to produce discussions and or ideas. Brainstorming is also a

great way to obtain a central topic for a project. In Chapter 2, we approached this concept by making lists of ideas and narrowing them down to what interests the writer enough to compose an entire paper. Not all people are list makers. Some alternatives might include:

- Collage- Get out those old markers and crayons. Find the glue sticks, glitter, and old magazines. Start your process with a central theme, probably one close to your paper's primary goal, and take it from there.
Consider the task from a creative standpoint. What do you want your readers to know? Why is it essential for your readers to know this? Furthermore, why are you qualified to show your readers this idea?
Sometimes to answer these questions, one just needs a clear mind.
- Doodles & Sketches - Like a collage, doodles and sketches take on new meaning when one puts the central goal to the forefront and leaves the dooming thought of developing a thesis stuck away. Take out a large piece of paper and write your target theme at the top. Start with a tight spiral in the upper left corner. This purpose is to clear your mind and, from there, begin to sketch out ideas. This might include small pictures or actual fragments of sentences. Maybe even a combination of the two.

Do this until the entire paper is covered. Using a different color pen or a highlighter, draw connections between those that are similar. The connections are the key because this helps a writer see what is there and what is missing.

- Mind Maps- This idea is a combination of a list and the sketch-doodle with words. Put your central theme in the middle of a piece of paper. Circle it. Now off of that circle, draw lines to whatever connections come to you. Draw more lines to connect to more narrow ideas. As you work your way through this, you will notice patterns emerging that form a narrower scope of your central idea, along with possible ways to illustrate this within a paper.

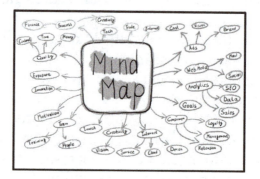

Organizing Thoughts

The methods in the last section could be used to organize your thoughts. In Chapter 3, we discussed outlining, yet not all outlines are the same.

- Post It Boards- For this, you will need a blank wall or sizeable whiteboard along with multi-colored post-it notes and markers. Use one color for your thesis and statements that describe or analyze other information around your thesis. A second color will feature each topic sentence for every subtopic you have developed. The next color will highlight quotes. Here you will write the exact quotation. To get the full effect of your resource, include the quote introduction. (This may be taken a step further by including the actual citation on the back to assist with producing your works cited page later on). Lastly, place your examples on different color backgrounds. Remember, research is based on logos, while (most) examples are based on pathos.

If a multi-colored post is not available, use a different color marker for each part. Moving either horizontally or vertically, place each topic sentence across the top. In the approximate order, the subtopic should be placed. Underneath, add your research and example. Finally, place the remaining post-its where appropriate. Remember, this shows how the previous work connects to your thesis.

EXAMPLE ILLUSTRATION

Consider your main goal. Do some of the subtopics need to be moved? Are there better possibilities to make your point? Where do you need to add or delete information? The color-coding also helps visualize if your paper is too example-heavy. A balanced argument is a good argument. Or the other way, do you have too many facts and stats and not enough emotional connections?

For this, you may be moving around more than subtopics. Resources may be appropriate in areas beyond where you are currently using them. Remember to review the connections you currently have. Do you need as or maybe you need a smaller lensed to back up a bit to get your readers to understand? Either way, this method is showing the big picture!

Communicating Ideas

As listed at the start of this chapter, we communicate ideas in many ways. This section features the results along with a simple checklist to take you there. Keep in mind that some steps, such as research, outline, and working thesis statements, are all positioned for multiple revisions along the way. Do not limit your process!

Poster Sessions

Possible steps to complete:

Idea > Research > Outline > Decisions > Rating information importance > Visuals > Word Choice > Revisions <> Layout <> Revisions <> layout > END RESULTS

Notice how, in several steps, the arrows point in both directions. At times, as writers, we need to take a step back to move forward.

PodCasts

Idea > Research > Outline > Script > Technology Choices >Tone >Music?> Practice <> Record <> Process > END RESULTS

Video

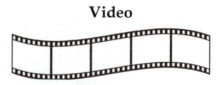

Idea > Research > Outline > Script <> Place/Time initial film< > Graphics?<> Visuals > Technology Choices <> Music?> Tone> Practice <> Record <> Process> END RESULTS.

Original Song/Spoken Word Poetry

Idea> Research> Outline> "visual"> "word choice" > Music choice> Length > Revise<> Practice <> record<> process> END RESULT,

Note that each starts with an idea, has some sort of research or development phase, revision takes place in almost every part of the process, and constantly evaluates methods and choices.

The most crucial consideration comes at the start; is this the most effective way to convey my message to my target audience?

Chapter Fourteen
Reflection

"THERE ARE THREE METHODS TO GAINING WISDOM. THE FIRST, REFLECTION, WHICH IS THE HIGHEST. THE SECOND, LIMITATION, WHICH IS THE EASIEST. AND THE THIRD, EXPERIENCE, WHICH IS THE BITTEREST."
CONFUCIUS

You thought you completed the assignment, correct?

You are close.

There is one last step to this whole writing process ordeal, and it is imperative to complete it. Beyond a grade or recognition, one may receive on a project, there is an absolute satisfaction in just completing the task.

Yes, I finished!

Sometimes this is a "yay me" high five over the head moment, and sometimes this is an "Oh fudge! I should have done that this way" confession.

In either situation, the writer reacts to their process, content, context, or something else within their prose.

Here is why we reflect.

We may ask ourselves the obvious question of what could we have done better?

Moreover, here there is always an answer because, as humans, we are our own worst critics, and it is easier to point out what went wrong. (I do not know why this is yet I am certain studies were done and reasons made).

Yes, we want to know where we can improve next time. Writing is a process, and like any other process, the more often you engage in the task, the better you will get.

Your first list may have a few suggestions to improve on next time. If your professor gives comments, consider those as well. Of course, your thoughts are important, too, because only you know the time and effort put into a project.

The next part is usually tricky for people; ask yourself what you did well. What are you most proud of? Again, if your professor wrote comments, you may have a few notes from their perspective yet, think about what you see as your best within this project.

Give yourself a "yay me high five" moment. Celebrating completing a task, especially a long, complex one, is necessary. We must focus on the ultimate goal and how we are one step closer to its achievement.

The last part of reflection takes you inward to ask what you learned throughout this process. Whether we are in the classroom or part of a corporate team, each project should have some sort of lesson at the end. (Think Aesop, "and the moral of the story is...")

Let us consider the following:

- What did you know about the topic/issue/subject before this project?

- What was your biggest challenge? How did you move past this challenge?
- Where did experience come into play? Did your past experiences help or hinder your progress?
- What do you wish you knew before starting?
- Finally, what did you add to the overall conversation on this subject? In other words, what did you bring to the table?

When we answer the previous questions, and possibly some of our own that developed, the process facilitates seeing beyond just the words on the paper.

Now, as a writer, you see how your work, your engagement "fits" into the overall big picture.

Yes, now you have completed The Funnel.

Exercise

✓ This one is simple. Let's think of reflection beyond our writing.

Consider a situation you could have handled better. This could be anything from a rude customer where you work or a dumb argument with a friend.

Review the situation on paper. What could you have done better? What will you change the next time this happens?

This, simply, is reflecting.

Chapter Fifteen
Real World
Applications

"PRACTICE EXECUTION BECOMES
GAME TIME REALITY."
JULIAN EDELMAN

One last thought

The process you just completed applies to other classwork. Writing a paper is writing a paper, right? *The Funnel* method may apply to any type of project to produce a well-researched, organized, thought-provoking end product.

We hinted at a real-life application in the last chapter, yet beyond reflecting, where can you use these methods?

In every career, some type of writing takes place. The social worker needs to document visits, the police traffic stops, and the computer programmer a process via email.

It all comes down to words on paper.

The Funnel may be used as a checklist to make sure all the details are present. It may also be tweaked to fit your career. For instance, if there is specific information that must appear in a report, why not turn each "subtopic" area into a prompt for that specific item. Here *The Funnel* becomes an organizing method.

The beauty part of this whole process is to make it your own, so it functions for what you need. The steps help in pushing a topic further and bringing new information to the forefront.

Best in your future writing, and remember to *Funnel It*!

References

Carillo, Ellen C. *A Guide To Mindful Reading.*
Boulder: University Press of Colorado,
2017. Book.

Courtney, Jennifer Pooler. "A Review of
Rewriting: How to do Things with Texts."
The Journal of Effective Teaching (2007): 74-77.
Document.

Duffy, John. "Radical Humilities: Post-Truth,
Ethics, and the Teaching of Writing." Storrs,
7 April 2017. Lecture.

—. "The Good Writer: Virtue Ethics and the
Teaching of Writing." *College English,*
January 2017: 229-250. Document.

Elbow, Peter. "Bringing the Rhetoric of Assent and
the Believing Game Together - and Into the
Classroom." *College English,* March 2005.
Document.

Harris, Joseph. *Rewriting: How to Do Things with
Texts.* August: Utah State University Press,
2017. Book.

Maxwell, Rebecca. *Spatial Orientation and the Brain: The Effects of Map Reading and Navigation.* 8 March 2013. Web. December 2018.

Stein, Vicky. *Why we still need paper maps.* 9 January 2019. Web. 15 January 2019.

Cover Art:

https://www.clipartmax.com/middle/m2i8i8d3m2N4b1N4_clip-art-tags-funnel-clip-art/

Acknowledgments

I am fortunate to be surrounded by giving, curious, resourceful people. From the start of this project on through final revisions, I had both peers and students who motivated me to continue. Those include Dr. Elizabeth Brewer-Olson, Dr. Melissa Mentzer, and Dr. Stephen Cohen of Central Connecticut State University; Dr. Mary Isbell, University of New Haven; Dr. Ellen Carillo of the University of Connecticut. And Lois Church, Stephanie Fischer, Kelly Jarvis, and Brendan Kelly.
I appreciate the time and energy my peer reviewers and editors took to make this project better. Mike Palmquist, Aimee Taylor, Karen-Elizabeth Moroski, and Aleashia Walton, thank you for your direction and patience.
My inspirations from long ago are part of every project I complete. They include Christine Archer, Kay Janney, Jamie Cat Callan, and Jim Parise, who, without their support, I would not be in academia. Other inspirations include:
Ms. Amanda Pampuro, for reading the entire draft on short notice. My Mom and Dad for a "world of possibilities," along with my husband Steve, and son, Enrico, for keeping me grounded.
Finally, thank you, thank you, thank you, to my writing students who inspire me daily to be a better teacher and a better human.
Peace.

Lynn M. Patarini (M.A.L.S. Wesleyan) has taught undergraduate composition and literature for over ten years at various colleges and universities. Teaching is a second career after an awarding winning 20+ years in media.

In addition to teaching, she is also the author of several novels under the pseudonym L.M. Pampuro. For more information on her creative side, visit Pampuro.com.

GRATEFUL
PUBLISHING

CPSIA information can be obtained
at www.ICGtesting.com
Printed in the USA
LVHW051700141121
703289LV00014B/1462